Let's Joke Around!

LET'S TELL JOKES ABOUT MONKEYS AND APES

Leonard Clasky

WINDMILL BOOKS

Published in 2023 by Windmill Books, an Imprint of Rosen Publishing
2544 Clinton St., Buffalo, NY 14224

Disclaimer: Portions of this work were originally authored by Maria Nelson and published as *Jokes and More About Monkeys and Apes*. All new material in this edition authored by Leonard Clasky.

Editor: Caitie McAneney
Book Design: Rachel Rising

Photo Credits: Cover jeep2499/Shutterstock.com; cover, pp. 1, 3-24 (background) V_ctoria/Shutterstock.com; p. 4 Eric Isselee/Shutterstock.com; p. 5 (bottom) Laure BAUDEMENT/Shutterstock.com; p. 5 (top) Yusnizam Yusof/Shutterstock.com; pp. 6, 8, 10, 12, 14, 16, 18, 20, 22 Vectors Bang/Shutterstock.com; p. 7 luckyraccoon/Shutterstock.com; p. 9 Marie Henson/Shutterstock.com; p. 11 Ivanova Ksenia/Shutterstock.com; p. 13 Anton Watman/Shutterstock.com; p. 15 Kittisak Srithorn/Shutterstock.com; p. 17 Photo Spirit/Shutterstock.com; p. 19 tamayura/Shutterstock.com; p. 21 JT Platt/Shutterstock.com.

Cataloging-in-Publication Data
Names:Clasky, Leonard.
Title: Let's tell jokes about monkeys and apes / Leonard Clasky.
Description: New York : Windmill Books, 2023. | Series: Lets's Joke Around!| Includes glossary.
Identifiers: ISBN 9781538392942 (pbk.) | ISBN 9781538392959 (library bound) | ISBN 9781538392966 (ebook)
Subjects: LCSH: Ape, humor –Juvenile literature. | Jokes –Juvenile literature. | Monkey, humor –Juvenile literature
Classification: LCC PN6231.M663 C53 2023 | DDC 818/.602–dc23

Manufactured in the United States of America

CPSIA Compliance Information: Batch #CWWM23. For further information contact Rosen Publishing at 1-800-237-9932.

Find us on

CONTENTS

MONKEY FUN

Have you ever heard the saying "more fun than a barrel of monkeys"? Monkeys and apes are amazing animals—with a silly side! They are **primates**—an animal group that also includes humans. Monkeys and apes are different from each other because monkeys have tails and are usually smaller than apes. Monkeys and apes are smart animals. They are also **social**. They're known to climb, play, and swing from trees. Now, stop monkeying around, and learn some funny jokes about monkeys and apes!

CHIMPANZEE

SOME MONKEYS EVEN LOOK A LITTLE FUNNY, WITH TOOTHY SMILES, MUSTACHES, AND SILLY NOSES!

PROBOSCIS MONKEY

EMPEROR TAMARIN

SNACK TIME!

WHAT IS AN APE'S FAVORITE FRUIT?
Ape-ricots.

WHAT DO APES EAT FOR DESSERT?
Chocolate chimp cookies.

WHAT DID THE APE BRING TO THE PARTY?
Chimps and dip.

WHY DO MONKEYS LOVE BANANAS? Because they have appeal.

TRAVELING MONKEYS

WHAT DO YOU CALL A MONKEY AT THE NORTH POLE?
Lost.

WHY DID THE MONKEY CROSS THE ROAD?
The chicken took the day off.

WHAT DID THE MONKEY SAY AFTER GETTING CAUGHT IN TRAFFIC?
"It's a jungle out there today!"

MONKEY TROUBLE!

WHY WAS THE HOWLER MONKEY SO LOUD?
He was born in a zoo.

WHAT WAS WRONG WITH THE SICK CHIMPANZEE?
He had a tummy-ape.

WHAT HAPPENS WHEN A MONKEY GETS FLEAS?
It's lunch time!

MONKEYS ON THE MOVE

WHAT HAPPENED WHEN THE MONKEY CHASED THE BANANA?
The banana split.

WHERE DO MONKEYS WORK OUT?
The jungle gym.

WHAT DID THE APE SAY TO HER LAZY SON?
"Stop monkeying around, and do your homework!"

13

MONKEY LOVE

WHAT DID THE CHIMP SAY TO HIS GIRLFRIEND?
"I go ape over you!"

WHERE CAN MONKEYS GO TO FIND LOVE?
Monkey bars!

WHICH MONTH IS THE BEST FOR A GORILLA WEDDING?
Ape-ril.

WHAT DID THE MONKEY CALL HIS WIFE?

His prime-mate.

MANY KINDS OF MONKEYS

WHAT DO YOU CALL A CROWD OF APES?
An orangutangle.

WHAT KIND OF MONKEY SOUNDS LIKE A SHEEP?
A baa-boon.

WHAT KIND OF MONKEY IS FOUND IN THE SEA?
A shrimpanzee.

WHAT DO YOU CALL A MONKEY WITH EIGHT LEGS?
A spider monkey.

WHAT DO YOU CALL AN ANGRY MONKEY?
Furious George!

WHAT DO YOU CALL A MONKEY WHO CAN'T KEEP A SECRET?
A blab-boon.

HOW DID THE APE GET DOWNSTAIRS SO QUICKLY?
He slid down the banana-ster.

WHAT'S A MONKEY'S FAVORITE CHRISTMAS SONG?
Jungle Bells.

MONKEYS ON THE JOB

WHAT DO YOU CALL A MONKEY IN CHARGE OF HER TREE?
The branch manager.

WHAT DID THE MONKEY CHEF WEAR TO WORK?
An ape-ron.

WHAT DO YOU CALL AN APE WHO WORKS IN A CALL CENTER?
A who-rang-utan.

FUN MONKEY AND APE FACTS!

- The male **proboscis** monkey has the largest nose of any primate. It's also known for being a great swimmer with belly-flop skills!

- Monkeys are split into two groups. Old World monkeys live in Africa and Asia, while New World monkeys live in the Americas.

- Howler monkeys have a loud call that can be heard about 2 to 3 miles (3.2 to 4.8 km) away!

- Monkeys and apes **groom** each other every day, which increases their social **bonds**, makes their fur healthy, and provides a buggy snack!

- With **opposable** thumbs, monkeys and apes can use tools and even play games.

GLOSSARY

bond: A feeling that brings people or animals together.

capuchin: A small Central or South American monkey with a nearly bare face and a "cap" of dark hair on its head.

groom: To make something neat or clean.

opposable: Capable of being placed against one or more of the remaining digits of a hand or foot.

primate: Any animal from the group that includes humans, apes, and monkeys.

proboscis: A long, flexible trunk or snout (body part including the nose, mouth, and jaws) on an animal.

social: Living in groups instead of alone.

FOR MORE INFORMATION

Books

Dahl, Michael. *Silly Jokes About Animals*. North Mankato, MN: Pebble Books, 2022.

Gottlieb, Beth. *I Love Monkeys!* New York, NY: Gareth Stevens Publishing, 2023.

Sexton, Colleen A. *Squirrel Monkey*. Minneapolis, MN: Bearport Publishing Company, 2023.

Websites

Monkeys

sdzwildlifeexplorers.org/animals/monkeys
Explore more about monkeys with the San Diego Zoo Wildlife Explorers.

10 Chimpanzee Facts

www.natgeokids.com/uk/discover/animals/general-animals/10-chimpanzee-facts/
Learn fun facts about chimpanzees with *National Geographic Kids*!